Do You Hear What I See?

Looking at the World in New Ways

Titles in This Set

Cover Artist

Steven Guarnaccia is a versatile artist and a well-known collector too. You can find his illustrations on masks, T-shirts, magazine covers, book jackets, and posters, as well as on book covers like this one. What does he collect? Rooster ties, among other things.

ISBN: 0-673-80045-8

Acknowledgments appear on page 144.

345678910RRS99989796959493

Do You Hear What I See?

Looking at the World in New Ways

ScottForesman

A Division of HarperCollins*Publishers*

Contents

Problem Solvers

Pencils, Paintbrushes, Needles and Thread (Genre Study)

The Amazing Glen Rounds
(Author/Illustrator Study)

Take a Closer Look

Student Resources

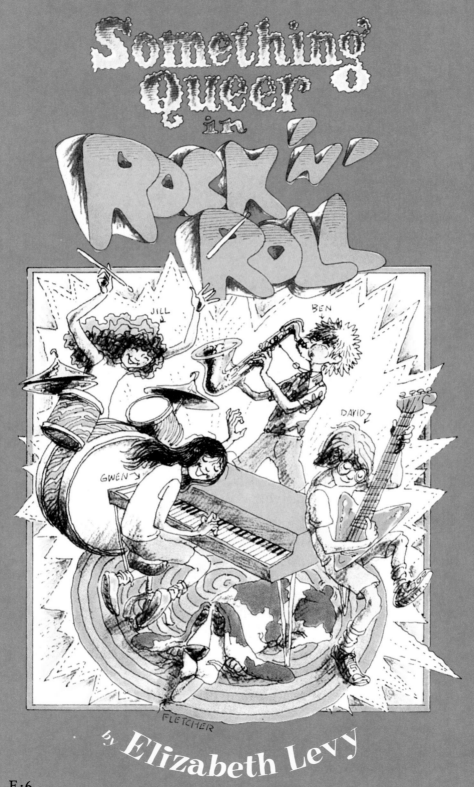

Something Queer in Rock 'n' Roll

by Elizabeth Levy

E·6

Gwen pounded the piano. Jill flipped her drumstick into the air. Ben's saxophone wailed, and David kept everything steady on the electric bass. Under the piano, Fletcher wagged his tail in time to the music. Gwen and Jill had recently joined a rock 'n' roll band.

"Did you hear about the TV rock contest?" said Gwen when they'd finished their song. "It's for kids under twelve."

"We've got to come up with an original song," said Jill.

"No problem," said Gwen.

But there was a problem.

The group argued over every note. Their music sounded so awful that Fletcher's tail stopped wagging. He put his paws over his ears.

"I'm starved," said Gwen finally. "I can't write another note if we don't eat something."

"Food might be a help," said Jill.

"Let's order pizza," said Ben. "Pizza with pepperoni."

"And extra cheese," said David.

"But no anchovies!" said Gwen.

When the pizza arrived Fletcher's nose twitched. He stood up on his hind legs, plunked his front paws on the piano keys, and howled.

Ben and David started laughing.

"Don't mind him," said Jill. "He's hungry all the time. It's a dog's life."

"That's it!" shouted Gwen. She played chords on the piano and sang. "It's a dog's life."

Suddenly the group wasn't arguing anymore. Within minutes they had written the words and a tune.

"Let's call ourselves Fletcher and the Gang," said Gwen.

"We can wear long ears," said David.

"We can give Fletcher a punk dog collar," said Ben.

"I'm not sure that Fletcher likes punk," said Jill.

"Let's just hope he keeps liking pizza," said Ben. "We need that final howl for the contest."

"Don't worry," said Gwen. "Fletcher will never get tired of pizza."

Fletcher and the Gang went to the TV station for the open auditions.

Hundreds of kids showed up in all sorts of costumes—punk rockers, Madonna look-alikes, young yuppies, and Elvis look-alikes. Nobody else had a dog.

Gwen, Jill, Ben, and David were very nervous. But when Jill held pizza over Fletcher's head, he howled on cue. Then the Gang joined in with a high-pitched "OWW . . . WOOO . . . WOOO . . . WOOOO."

The judges all laughed.

One week later they found out they were finalists. The TV station wanted them at a dress rehearsal on Wednesday.

They decided to practice every day after school.

The next day Jill showed up for rehearsal looking panic-stricken. "Fletcher's missing!" she cried.

"Maybe he found a girlfriend," joked David. "Maybe he's got his first groupie."

"This isn't funny," insisted Gwen.

Gwen tapped her braces.

"Why is she doing that?" demanded Ben and David.

"Because something queer is going on," said Gwen. "Fletcher wouldn't just disappear."

They searched the neighborhood. There was no sign of Fletcher.

Gwen, Jill, Ben, and David put up posters all over town offering a reward. Nobody called.

"We're ruined," said Ben. "Without Fletcher's final note, we're nothing."

"I'd give up fame and fortune just to have Fletcher back," said Jill in tears.

Gwen put her arm around Jill. "We have to go to the rehearsal. Fletcher would have wanted us to carry on."

On the night of the rehearsal, Fletcher was still missing. The other finalists had terrific costumes. The Baroos were dressed as mummies.

The Tarantulas had spider suits and wore webbed masks.

The Potatoes had costumes that covered their bodies. Each one was a different kind of potato.

The Teeny-Weeny Boppers wore clown makeup. The lead singer, Willie, was only five; Risa was tiny, but she banged out a mean sound on her toy xylophone.

"We look silly in our Fletcher ears without a dog to howl," grumbled David.

"Where's the dog?" muttered the director. "He was the best thing in your act."

Gwen sighed. "He just wandered off."

"That's rock 'n' roll for you," said the director.

The following day Gwen, Jill, Ben, and David tried to rehearse, but nobody's heart was in it.

Then the phone rang.

"If you want your dog back, go to Durant and Original," said a squeaky high voice.

"Who is this?" Jill demanded.

The caller hung up.

Gwen and Jill ran to the corner of Durant and Original. The street was deserted.

"Look!" Gwen said. She pointed to one of their reward signs for Fletcher taped onto a lamppost. A red arrow pointed to an empty lot. It looked like it had been drawn in blood.

Suddenly they heard a whimper.

"Fletcher!" cried Jill.

CLOSE-UP OF THE ARROW

Fletcher was standing in a pile of garbage, surrounded by newspapers, empty pizza boxes, and pop bottles.

Gwen touched the arrow on the lamppost. "It's sticky, maybe it's blood. Is Fletcher cut?"

Jill felt Fletcher all over. "He's a little thin, but I can't find any blood."

They carried Fletcher back to Jill's house.

"Look at this," cried Jill. A piece of light brown felt hung from Fletcher's collar.

"A clue!" exclaimed Gwen.

"What's she, an amateur detective?" asked David.

"Gwen's very good at solving mysteries," said Jill.

"Let's order pizza," said Ben. "Fletcher has to practice his howl."

When the pizza was delivered Fletcher hid under the piano. Jill put a slice under his nose. Fletcher wasn't interested! He wouldn't howl. He hated pizza.

"We're ruined!" exclaimed David.

"Sabotage!" said Gwen with a tap to her braces. "I knew there was something queer about Fletcher's disappearance."

"Maybe he's just tired from his ordeal," said Jill. "We'll try again tomorrow."

On Thursday they ordered pizza. Fletcher hid behind the drums.

They tried on Friday. Fletcher ran out of the room when he smelled pizza.

Gwen tapped her braces. "The fiend who

THE STICKY ARROW   THE SCRAP OF BROWN FELT

force-fed Fletcher cut himself or herself, and wrote
the arrow in blood. He or she was also wearing light
brown felt. I want to visit each of the other finalists.
They all had a motive. Besides, Fletcher might growl
if he sees his fiendish feeder."

They took Fletcher to see the Tarantulas, who
had added silver studs to their spider costumes.

"Anybody need a Band-Aid?" asked Gwen.

The lead spider gave Gwen a dirty look. "Hey, your dog reminds me of Bruce Springroll," he said.

Fletcher wagged his tail at the fuzzy spider costumes.

"I don't think it's them," whispered Jill.

Next they visited the Potatoes. Mashed Potato was in a foul mood because their lead singer, French Fry, wasn't there.

"He's always late," complained Boiled Potato.

Gwen looked down at Fletcher for any sign of fear.

He had fallen asleep on Baked Potato's drum pedal.

At the Baroos', Fletcher grabbed an end of a mummy wrap and started to pull.

Gwen tapped her braces. Was one of the mummies bandaged to hide a cut?

"Are you all wrapped up as mummies so you don't cut yourself again?" asked Gwen.

"Nobody has a cut," said Ellen, the lead Baroo.

Fletcher wagged his tail.

"It's not the Baroos," said Jill. "Let's get out of here before we're all wrapped up."

Willie of Teeny-Weeny Boppers had on a baseball cap. He hugged Fletcher. "Cute doggie," said Willie.

Fletcher licked his face, then he gave tiny Risa a kiss.

"He likes us," said Willie.

"Great," moaned Jill.

Sunday arrived—the day of the live TV show—
and Fletcher still wouldn't howl for pizza. Gwen was
no closer to finding out who had taken him.

"We're gonna bomb," said David.

Gwen, Jill, Ben, and David put on their
hound-dog ears and dog collars.

"Don't worry," said Gwen. "Fletcher and I
won't let you down."

The rest of the group groaned.

On the way to the TV station, they stopped at
the pizza parlor. They ordered a pizza.

Gwen tapped her braces. "Has anybody been order-
ing a shocking number of pizzas?" she asked the owner.

"I'll say," said the owner. "Business has been
booming."

"Can you give us the address of your best
customer?" asked Gwen. "It's important."

"Well, I don't know what harm it will do." She
handed Gwen a slip of paper.

"That's our address," said Jill.

"You've been our best customer, right?" The
owner turned to the kid who had been delivering
pizzas to Jill's house.

Fletcher whimpered. He hated pizza!

"Aren't you going to be late again?" the owner asked the kid.

Gwen tapped her braces.

Gwen and Jill took the pizza to the TV station. Gwen looked around for the Potatoes. Boiled was dressed like a new red potato. Baked was wrapped in aluminum foil. French Fry showed up at the last minute in a brown felt costume with cut-out holes for his eyes and mouth.

"I gotta see the poster with the arrow," said Gwen.

Jill dug it out of her knapsack.

Gwen licked the dried-up red arrow.

"Yuk," said Jill.

"It's tomato sauce," said Gwen. "Not blood."
Gwen picked up the piece of brown felt she had found
on Fletcher's dog collar.

Gwen walked up to the boy dressed as a french
fry. Sure enough, there was a patch on the back of his
costume.

"Excuse me," said Gwen. "Does this belong
to you?" Gwen showed French Fry the piece of
brown felt.

"Where did you find that?" asked French Fry.

"On Fletcher's dog collar!" yelled Jill.

French Fry ran off the stage.

Gwen and Jill chased him, knocking over one of
the spiders, unwrapping one of the Baroo mummies.
Fletcher flew after the fleeing fiendish French Fry.

Finally Gwen flipped the pizza at French Fry.
He slipped in the gooey cheese and fell on the floor.

Jill tackled him. "I've got the rotten potato," she cried. She had tomato sauce and cheese all over her arms.

"What's going on here?" demanded the director of the TV show.

"Something queer in rock 'n' roll," said Gwen. "That's what's going on!"

French Fry took off the top of his costume. He was the boy who delivered pizza to the house.

"I knew it was you," said Gwen.

"Tell us why you did what you did," said Jill, sitting on French Fry. "Or I'll stuff your mouth with pizza the way you did to Fletcher."

"I knew you got that special sound from that dumb dog," said French Fry. "I watched you rehearse when I delivered pizza. Your dog loves pizza. I hid him in the basement of the pizza parlor and fed him pizzas so he'd get sick of them. But he got so lonely for his owners that he wouldn't eat. I let him go."

"Yeah, but you ruined our song," said Gwen. "Fletcher hates pizza now. He's not hungry all the time."

The director looked frazzled. "French Fry, you're out of the show," he said. "As for the rest of you, we're on live in fifteen minutes."

"Now what?" asked Jill. "Fletcher still hates pizza!"

"Just put on your ears, and pray," said Gwen.

Fletcher and the Gang went onstage, and Fletcher was front and center. But would he howl?

Gwen patted him on the head. "I know you hate pizzas, but how about a bite of salami?" she whispered.

Gwen held a tiny piece of salami over Fletcher's head.

Fletcher lifted his head and howled, "OWW . . . WOOO. . . WOOO. . . WOOOO."
  "It's a dog's life."

Fletcher and the Gang won the contest paws down.

"Hungry All the Time"

Words by Elizabeth Levy   Music by Ben Harris

A (Chorus)

Hun-gry all the time_____ That's just like a dog's life
Wait-ing for pizza's a crime That's just like a dog's life

That's just like a dog's life_____
That's just like a dog's life_____

B (Verse)   D. S. al **A**

Hold the an-cho-vies They smell just like old sto-gies
Don't want no sword fish Don't go well in my dog dish

(Repeat Chorus)
Verse (Repeat Music B)

Want a salami mummy
To pat me on the tummy
Don't want no macaroni
Just pizza and pepperoni

C (Verse)

I'm_____ no_____ pus-sy-cat Not a-fraid of be-ing fat

D. S. al **A**

I'm not built for chas-ing rats I'm_____ a dog who's

(Chorus)
Hungry all the time
That's just like a dog's life
Waiting for pizza's a crime
That's just like a dog's life
OWW..WOOO...WOOO...WOOOO!

Thinking About It

1. When did you first figure out the solution to the mystery? Did you solve it before Gwen?

2. You are Fletcher. Tell what happened to you after your group became one of the finalists.

3. And now, making their first music video, we present the rockin'est rollin'est group of today! That's you! What would you name a rock 'n' roll group? What makes your group a winner?

Another Book by Elizabeth Levy

Gwen and Jill are at it again! Jill plans a surprise party for Gwen, but the invitations, presents, and even the birthday cake disappear. Can the girls crack this case? Find out in *Something Queer at the Birthday Party.*

THE CROW AND THE PITCHER

retold by Tom Paxton

"I'm dying of thirst!" cawed the crow in despair.
He looked in a pitcher—some water was there!
He stuck in his beak for a drink, but—hello—
It seemed that the level of water was low.
His beak couldn't reach it,
His chances looked slim,
But then an idea came leaping at him.
He picked up a pebble, flew back in a flash;
It dropped in the pitcher and fell with a splash.
Again and again came the black-feathered flier.
Each pebble that fell brought the sweet water higher.
At last, when the water was near to the brink,
This quick-thinking bird took a well-deserved drink.
So wisdom informs us in this little rhyme,
That little by little will work every time.

How to Weigh an Elephant

retold by Frances Alexander

A Chinese Emperor of the Wei Kingdom was presented an elephant by one of his subjects. He gave his ministers three days to tell him the weight of the elephant. If they could not tell him, they would lose their heads.

The ministers had only small scales. How could they weigh such a large creature? They worked hard to find the answer. By the third day they were sure they would lose their heads.

But Prince Chung, a young boy, declared that he could weigh the elephant. A great crowd gathered at the water's edge as the young prince had the elephant placed on a boat. The prince then swam around the boat marking the water line with red paint.

Then the elephant was removed and the boat filled with stones until it sank to the red water line. The boy weighed the stones one by one, added the weights together, and found the weight of the elephant.

Thus Prince Chung saved the heads of the ministers and gained great favor with the Emperor of Wei.

BO RABBIT
SMART FOR TRUE

retold by Priscilla Jaquith
illustrations by Ed Young

One morning at first-day, Elephant was just lying down in his bed on the high hill when . . .

"Wait, Elephant! Wait!" cries a voice under his right leg.

Elephant holds his leg heist in the air. "Who's that?"

"It's me." Bo Rabbit hops out. "Why don't you watch what you do, Elephant? You almost mash me."

"You're too little," grumbles Elephant. "Nobody can see you."

"Little! I'm not too little. You're too big. You're one big man, Elephant." He watches Elephant stretch out in his bed. "You're even more big lying down than standing up."

"I know. I'm the biggest thing on earth, Bo Rabbit."

"Elephant, you know one thing? If I wanted to, big as you are and little as I am, I could pull you right out your bed."

"What kind of talk you talking, Rabbit? I'm up all night. I come here for catch some sleep and you have to come botheration me about pull me out my bed. Go 'long and let me sleep."

"Elephant, if I'm nigh you so your bigness scares me, I can't do it, for true. But if you let me tie one rope to you and get back in the brush where I can't see you, I bet I can pull you right out your bed."

"You couldn't move one of my ears, Rabbit."

"But if I do, Elephant, if I do, you never say I'm too little then, isn't it so?"

"All right, all right. Go away now."

Bo Rabbit takes his departure. He walks on and walks on, *kapot, kapot, kapot,* through the brush and down the hill till he reaches the ocean shore.

Far out in the blue, he sees Whale swimming.

"Hi there, Whale," he hollers.

Whale spouts, *Szi, Szi, Szi,* and leaps high to look

towards shore. Then he swims close and pulls up with a great swish of his tail, SPASHOW.

"G'morning, Bo Rabbit."

"Where you been, Whale? I ain't seen you in a long time."

"I been clean around the earth, Rabbit."

"Gracious, Whale, you sure do grow to be one big man."

"I know. I'm the biggest thing in the water, Rabbit."

"Whale, you know one thing?"

"What, Bo Rabbit?"

"Little as I am and big as you are, if I wanted to, I could pull you right out the Salt."

Whale laughs till he splutters, *Shuplu, shuplu, shuplu.* "What kind of talk you talking, Rabbit? You couldn't *move* me in the ocean, let alone pull me out. You're too little."

"Oh, no, I'm not. If I'm there when you come out the water so your bigness scares me, I can't do it, for true. But if you let me tie one rope to you so I can go back on the hill where I can't see you, I bet I can pull you right out the sea. You never call me too little then, isn't it so?"

"All right, all right. I like to see that, Rabbit. I surely would."

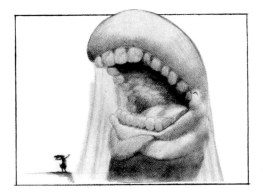

Bo Rabbit goes home and gets a long rope.

Then he takes his foot in his hand and runs to Elephant's house.

Elephant is in his bed asleep. Bo Rabbit yells, "Roll over, Elephant. Roll over."

Elephant stirs. Bo Rabbit slings the rope around him in one big loop.

"Elephant," he hollers, "when you feel me pull, you pull hard as you can, hear?"

"All right." Elephant goes back to sleep.

Bo Rabbit takes the other end of the rope and runs down hill to the shore where Whale is waiting.

"Hey, Whale, come close as you can, will you? I like to tie this rope around you."

Whale comes close and Bo Rabbit ties the knot tight.

"Whale, when you feel me pull, you pull hard as you can, hear?"

"All right, Rabbit."

Bo Rabbit goes in the middle of the rope and he takes it in all two his hands and he pulls from all two

ends one time, *hrup,
hrup, hrup.*

Elephant, asleep in his
bed, doesn't have Bo
Rabbit in the back part of
his head, but Whale is
waiting in the water for

see what Bo Rabbit will do.

When he feels Bo Rabbit make his pull, he gives a
big jerk, KPUT.

The first thing Elephant knows, he's jerked out his
bed and goes sumbleset down the hill, *fahlip, fahlip,
fahlip.*

He can't get on his foot. When he does, he starts to
pull, *hrup, hrup, hrup.* But all he can pull, he keeps

going to the sea.

Except he see two trees
and brace himself against
them, Whale would have
pulled him clean into the
sea and drowned him.

But all Whale pull,
hrup, hrup, hrup, he can't

pull Elephant out of those trees.

By and by in the sun-hot, Whale gets tired. He
gives slack back on the rope and Elephant takes that
slack up the hill and pulls Whale clean out of the deep.

Except Whale hold onto a rock in the Salt,
Elephant would have pulled him all the way to the
high hill. But hard as Elephant pull, *hrup, hrup, hrup,*
he can't pull Whale out of the sea.

By and by in the sun-hot, Elephant gets tired. He gives back slack. Whale gives a jerk, KPUT, and pulls till he's back in the deep.

Bo Rabbit chuckles and takes out his pocket knife.

Directly Whale gets tired and Elephant goes back on the hill, Bo Rabbit slips out and cuts the rope in the middle, *sazip, sazip, sazip.*

Then he grabs the end of the rope tied to Elephant and runs after him.

"What you say now, Elephant?" he cries, dancing around him and waving the rope in the air. "What you say now? You're not in your bed, are you? I pulled you right out of it, didn't I? Didn't I?"

Elephant looks at the rope in Bo Rabbit's hand. "How do you do it, Bo Rabbit? Little as you are and big as I am, how do you do it?"

"I'm one able little man, Elephant. But I'm not too little, am I? Say I'm not too little or I jerk you right over my head and throw you in the sea and drown you for true."

"You're not too little," Elephant is hasty to say.

"All right. You can go now."

"So long, Bo Rabbit. Maybe I get some sleep at

last." Elephant lumbers off to bed.

Bo Rabbit runs down hill and picks up the end of the rope tied to Whale. Then he goes to the shore where Whale is waiting.

"What you say now, Whale?" he cries, dancing up and down and waving the rope in the air. "I pulled you clean out the deep, didn't I? Didn't I?"

Whale spouts, *szi, szi, szi,* and looks at the rope in Bo Rabbit's hand. "How do you do it, Bo Rabbit? Little as you are and big as I am, how do you do it?"

"I'm one able little man, Whale. But I'm not too

little, am I? Say I'm not too little or I jerk you right over my head and throw you up on the high hill."

"You're not too little, Rabbit." Whale slaps the sea with his tail for emphasis, SPASHOW. "If you're any bigger, you can move the earth and flood the world and nobody be safe. Oh, no, you're not too little, Bo Rabbit. Not too little, at all."

No matter how little you are, if you're smart for true, you can best the biggest crittuh in the sea and the biggest crittuh on earth. It stands so.

THINKING ABOUT IT

1. The crow, Prince Chung, and Bo Rabbit are all "smart for true." Prove it! How did each one show he was smart?

2. There's a lesson to be learned in each story. Which lesson makes the most sense to you? Tell why you think so.

3. Choose one of the characters and make up a new problem for that character to solve. Make sure the crow, Prince Chung, or Bo Rabbit use their wits to solve the problem.

CHARACTERS:
SCOOP SNOOPINS, *finder of lost characters*
ZELLA COURT, *his trusted secretary*
MRS. DUMPTY
MRS. COBBLER   } *clients*
MRS. PIPER

TIME: *The present.*
SETTING: *Scoop Snoopins's office. His desk is center—it has a phone, bulging file folders, telephone books, maps of the city, etc. Chairs for clients are up right of desk. File cabinets are left. Two trench coats and a hat are on coat tree, up right, and exit is right.*

AT RISE: SCOOP SNOOPINS *is busy at his desk when phone rings. He answers.*
SCOOP *(Into phone)*: Scoop Snoopins Lost and Found Detective Agency. May I help you? *(Reaching for paper and pencil)* Uh-huh. . . . Uh-huh. . . . O.K., Mr. Hubbard, let's take this from the top. *(Writing)* You say your wife went to the cupboard this morning? . . . And why did she do that? . . . To get your dog a bone. I see. Then what happened, Mr. Hubbard? . . . The cupboard was bare, hmm? . . . And that's when she disappeared? Well, this may be just a shot in the dark, but is it possible that she went to the grocery store? I may be totally wrong, of course, but from what you've told me, the evidence seems to be pointing in that direction. The missing station

wagon, the missing checkbook, the cents-off coupons missing from the food section of the paper all seem to indicate that shopping was on her mind. (ZELLA *enters and hangs up coat.*) Well, listen, Mr. Hubbard, if she's not back in an hour, call me and we'll take it from there. No problem—any time. (*Hangs up, looks at* ZELLA) Morning, Zella.

ZELLA: Morning, Scoop. You're here early.

SCOOP: Looks as if it's going to be a busy day. (*Hands her folders*) Do you mind wrapping up the paperwork on the Curds and Whey Affair?

ZELLA (*Pleased*): So you found out why the Muffet Girl ran away?

SCOOP (*Nodding*): Thanks to the anonymous tip about those spiders on Tuffets Landing. Seems that one sat down beside Miss Muffet and scared her out of her wits. She's O.K. now. (MRS. DUMPTY, *carrying purse, rushes in.*)

MRS. DUMPTY: Oh, thank goodness you're here!

SCOOP: Can we help you?

MRS. DUMPTY: I'm missing someone.

ZELLA: Then you've come to the right place.

SCOOP: Who is missing, ma'am?

MRS. DUMPTY: My husband. One minute, he was just sitting on the garden wall and in the very next, he was gone!

SCOOP (*Gesturing toward chair*): Why don't you have a seat, Mrs. . . .

MRS. DUMPTY: Dumpty. Mrs. H. Dumpty. (*Sits*)

SCOOP (*Taking notes*): What's your husband's name, Mrs. Dumpty?

MRS. DUMPTY: Humpty. Middle initial "A," for Arnold.

ZELLA: Do you have a picture of him?

MRS. DUMPTY: Right here in my purse. (*Takes photo from purse, hands it to* ZELLA) I took it last Easter.

SCOOP: Hm-m-m. He looks like a good egg to me . . . not the sort to run off.

MRS. DUMPTY: I'm so upset . . . I don't know what to do!

SCOOP: Just start with the facts, ma'am.

MRS. DUMPTY: Well, it was a hot day, so hot you could fry eggs on the sidewalk. Humpty was sitting outside, talking to the neighbors, and—(*Sobs*)

ZELLA (*Patting her shoulder*): There, there, don't go to pieces. If anyone can find your husband, it's Scoop Snoopins.

SCOOP: She's right, Mrs. Dumpty—I've unscrambled some of the toughest. Now, this may be a hard case to crack, but don't worry about a thing.

MRS. DUMPTY: But what if something terrible happened? What if he took a bad fall?

SCOOP: Well, he may be shell-shocked for a while, but—

ZELLA: Excuse me, Mrs. Dumpty, but did you check the other side of the wall?

MRS. DUMPTY (*Sobbing*): No.

ZELLA: Isn't it possible he could have simply rolled off?

MRS. DUMPTY: An egg roll? Yes, I suppose it's entirely possible.

SCOOP: Well, then, I suggest you put in a call immediately to all the king's horses and all the king's men. (*Aside; grimly*) You may need them.

MRS. DUMPTY (*Shaking her head*): I told those children that trampoline was dangerous.

ZELLA *and* SCOOP (*Puzzled*): Trampoline?

MRS. DUMPTY: The children next door always push their trampoline right up against our garden wall. (*Sighs*) Humpty might have landed on it, and who knows where he went from there, except up.

ZELLA (*Brightening*): And what goes up has to come down. Which means that he's all right.

SCOOP: As long as he keeps his sunny side up.

MRS. DUMPTY: Do you think he'll be back?

SCOOP: Eventually.

MRS. DUMPTY (*Shaking his hand*): Thank you, Mr. Snoopins. You really are a wizard. (*Exits*)

MRS. COBBLER (*Entering*): Is this the Scoop Snoopins Agency?

SCOOP: Sure is. How can we help you? (*Gestures to chair*) Please, have a seat.

MRS. COBBLER (*Crossing to sit down*): It's my children.

ZELLA: Are they lost?

MRS. COBBLER: I'm not sure. (*Upset*) You see, I have so many of them, I don't know what to do.

SCOOP: Let's start from the beginning. First of all, what's your name?

MRS. COBBLER: Mrs. Eunice Cobbler. I live in the large shoe at the end of the block.

ZELLA: Oh, yes, I've noticed it several times. Very unusual. Pointed toes are really in this season.

MRS. COBBLER: Thank you. Anyway, I have all these children—so many of them, I've totally lost count.

SCOOP: Is that so?

MRS. COBBLER: That's why I'm not sure if I'm missing any. There's Harry and Larry and Mary and Jerry and Terry and Barry and Gary and Perry and Carrie and—

SCOOP: Excuse me, but—(MRS. COBBLER *takes audible deep breath and continues, counting with fingers.*)

MRS. COBBLER: Teddy and Freddie and Nettie and Betty and Cal and Sal and Val and Al—

ZELLA: That's a lot of children!

MRS. COBBLER: You're telling me! It's impossible to keep track of them.

SCOOP: I can see why. Have you considered making a list?

MRS. COBBLER *(Snapping fingers)*: Bless my soul! I never thought of that!

ZELLA: You might also want to have them fingerprinted. The police department has a program that makes it easier to keep children safe and sound, whether you have one or a dozen.

MRS. COBBLER: How can I ever thank you?

SCOOP: Forget it. This advice is on the house.

MRS. COBBLER: Oh, thank you so much! (MRS. COBBLER *exits.*)

MRS. PIPER *(Entering)*: Pardon me, but do I need an appointment?

ZELLA: Not at all. Come on in.

ALL IN A DAY'S WORK.

MRS. PIPER (*Sitting*): I'm Mrs. Piper.

SCOOP: Is your husband Peter Piper?

MRS. PIPER (*Surprised*): Why, yes! Have you heard of him?

SCOOP: He made all the papers last week. Remember, Zella?

ZELLA: Oh, yes, the man who picked some peppers?

SCOOP: Pickled peppers, weren't they?

MRS. PIPER: A peck of them, to be precise.

ZELLA: What's your problem, Mrs. Piper?

MRS. PIPER: Peter seems to have disappeared.

ZELLA: Maybe all the publicity was too much for him.

MRS. PIPER: Possibly. Peter's a pretty private person.

SCOOP: We'll make finding him our priority, Mrs. Piper. I promise.

ZELLA: By the way, where's the peck of pickled peppers Peter Piper picked?

MRS. PIPER: Come to think of it, that's missing too.

SCOOP (*Puzzled*): This case sounds very confusing.

ZELLA: Wait a minute. Do you think Peter took his peppers to the county fair? That would be a perfect place to present his peppers to the public.

MRS. PIPER: I never thought of the fair! Of course! I'll go there on my way home. (*Exits*)

SCOOP (*To* ZELLA; *in admiration*): You're absolutely amazing.

ZELLA (*Shrugging*): All in a day's work.

SCOOP: No, I mean it, Zella. Your ideas are fantastic. What would I do without you?

ZELLA: Well, as the duck said when he didn't have enough cash, "Just put it on my bill." *(Takes files to cabinet)*

SCOOP: Humor aside, Zella, you're efficient, organized, perceptive, talented—I guess I just realized how lost I'd be without you!

ZELLA *(Checking her watch)*: Better not lose out on your next appointment.

SCOOP: Gosh—am I supposed to be somewhere?

ZELLA *(Helping him on with his coat)*: At the docks, remember? Captain Hanover's beautiful pea green boat was stolen last night.

SCOOP: Any suspects?

ZELLA: The crew said they've seen a suspicious-looking owl and a pussycat hanging around the marina.

SCOOP *(Helping her on with her coat)*: Did they get anything besides the boat?

ZELLA: They took some honey and plenty of money wrapped up in a five pound note.

SCOOP *(As they walk toward door)*: You'd better notify the Coast Guard.

ZELLA: I took care of it as soon as the call came in.

SCOOP *(Smiling)*: You're terrific, Zella. I think I've lost my heart!

ZELLA: Good news. *(Straightening his lapels)* I just found it. *(Gives him quick hug, exits; he smiles broadly, puts on his hat and follows her out. Curtain)*

THE END

1 If you were Scoop Snoopins's trusted assistant, what would you do to help him in his detective work?

2 What characters from Mother Goose did you find in the play? Read their speeches and see if people recognize them.

3 Scoop Snoopins and his assistant, Zella, have just gotten a new, really tough case to crack. What is it? What steps do they take to solve this new mystery?

Family Pictures

Cuadros de familia

written and illustrated by
Carmen Lomas Garza

*The pictures in this book are all painted from my
memories of growing up in Kingsville, Texas, near the
border with Mexico. From the time I was a young girl
I always dreamed of becoming an artist. I practiced
drawing every day; I studied art in school; and I
finally did become an artist. My family has inspired
and encouraged me for all these years. This is my book
of family pictures.*

*Los cuadros de este libro los pinté de los recuerdos de
mi niñez en Kingsville, Texas, cerca de la frontera con
México. Desde que era pequeña, siempre soñé con ser
artista. Dibujaba cada día; estudié arte en la escuela;
y por fin, me hice artista. Mi familia me ha inspirado
y alentado todos estos años. Éste es mi libro de cuadros
de familia.*

Birthday Party

 That's me hitting the piñata at my sixth birthday party. It was also my brother's fourth birthday. My mother made a big birthday party for us and invited all kinds of friends, cousins, and neighborhood kids.

You can't see the piñata when you're trying to hit it, because your eyes are covered with a handkerchief. My father is pulling the rope that makes the piñata go up and down. He will make sure that everybody has a chance to hit it at least once. Somebody will end up breaking it, and that's when all the candies will fall out and all the kids will run and try to grab them.

Cumpleaños

Ésa soy yo, pegándole a la piñata en la fiesta que me dieron cuando cumplí seis años. Era también el cumpleaños de mi hermano, que cumplía cuatro años. Mi madre nos dio una gran fiesta e invitó a muchos primos, vecinos y amigos.

No puedes ver la piñata cuando le estás dando con el palo, porque tienes los ojos cubiertos con un pañuelo. Mi padre está tirando de la cuerda que sube y baja la piñata. Él se encargará de que todos tengan por lo menos una oportunidad de pegarle a la piñata. Luego alguien acabará rompiéndola, y entonces todos los caramelos que tiene dentro caerán y todos los niños correrán a cogerlos.

E·51

Picking Nopal Cactus

 In the early spring my grandfather would come and get us and we'd all go out into the woods to pick nopal cactus. My grandfather and my mother are slicing off the fresh, tender leaves of the nopal and putting them in boxes. My grandmother and my brother Arturo are pulling leaves from the mesquite tree to line the boxes. After we got home my grandfather would shave off all the needles from each leaf of cactus. Then my grandmother would parboil the leaves in hot water. The next morning she would cut them up and stir fry them with chili powder and eggs for breakfast.

Piscando nopalitos

Al comienzo de la primavera, mi abuelo nos venía a buscar y todos íbamos al bosque a piscar nopalitos. Mi abuelo y mi madre están cortando las pencas tiernas del nopal y metiéndolas en cajas. Mi abuela y mi hermano Arturo están recogiendo hojas de mesquite para forrar las cajas. Después que regresábamos a casa, mi abuelo le quitaba las espinas a cada penca del cactus. Luego mi abuela cocía las pencas en agua hirviente. A la mañana siguiente, las cortaba y las freía con chile y huevos para nuestro desayuno.

Hammerhead Shark

 This picture is about the times my family went to Padre Island in the Gulf of Mexico to go swimming. Once when we got there, a fisherman had just caught a big hammerhead shark at the end of the pier. How he got the shark to the beach, I never found out. It was scary to see because it was big enough to swallow a little kid whole.

Tiburón martillo

Este cuadro trata de las veces que mi familia iba a nadar a la Isla del Padre en el Golfo de México. Una vez cuando llegamos, un pescador acababa de atrapar a un tiburón martillo al cabo del muelle. Cómo logró llevar al tiburón a la playa, nunca me enteré. Daba mucho miedo ver al tiburón, porque era tan grande que hubiera podido tragarse a un niño pequeño de un solo bocado.

Joseph and Mary
Seeking Shelter at the Inn

 On each of the nine nights before Christmas we act out the story of Mary and Joseph seeking shelter at the inn. We call this custom "Las Posadas." A little girl and a little boy play Mary and Joseph and they are led by an angel.

Each night the travelers go to a different house. They knock on the door. When the door opens, they sing: "We are Mary and Joseph looking for shelter." At first the family inside refuses to let them in; then the travelers sing again. At last Joseph and Mary are let into the house. Then everybody comes in and we have a party.

Las Posadas

Cada una de las nueve noches antes de Nochebuena, representamos la historia de María y José buscando albergue en la posada. Esta costumbre se llama "Las Posadas." Una niñita y un niñito representan a María y José, y hay un ángel que los guía.

Cada noche, los caminantes van a una casa distinta. Tocan la puerta. Cuando la puerta se abre, cantan: —Somos María y José, buscando posada. Al principio la familia no los deja entrar; entonces los caminantes vuelven a cantar. Por fin dejan entrar a María y José. Luego todos entran y celebran con una fiesta.

Beds for Dreaming

 My sister and I used to go up on the roof on summer nights and just stay there and talk about the stars and the constellations. We also talked about the future. I knew since I was thirteen years old that I wanted to be an artist. And all those things that I dreamed of doing as an artist, I'm finally doing now. My mother was the one who inspired me to be an artist. She made up our beds to sleep in and have regular dreams, but she also laid out the bed for our dreams of the future.

Camas para soñar

Mi hermana y yo solíamos subirnos al techo en las noches de verano y nos quedábamos allí platicando sobre las estrellas y las constelaciones. También platicábamos del futuro. Yo sabía desde que tenía trece años que quería ser artista. Y todas las cosas que soñaba hacer como artista, por fin las estoy haciendo ahora. Mi madre fue la que me inspiró a ser artista. Ella nos tendía las camas para que durmiéramos y tuviéramos sueños normales, pero también preparó la cuna para nuestros sueños del futuro.

Thinking About It

1. Imagine that you could step into one of Carmen Lomas Garza's paintings. Which one would you choose? What would you do there?

2. Carmen Lomas Garza describes what is going on in each one of her paintings. Choose one of the scenes in *Family Pictures*. Add to Ms. Lomas's description by telling what else you see in the painting.

3. Think of all the ways you could show people some things about your family. Which way would you choose? Would you make a statue or a quilt? Would you write a play? Would you do something else? What information about your family would you like people to know?

FAITH RINGGOLD'S STORIES IN ART

by Leslie Sills

Some people tell stories. Faith Ringgold paints them—and sews them. Using needles, thread, beads, and fabrics of all kinds, Ringgold makes masks, puppets, and quilts that tell stories about her family and the African American community in which she lives.

Faith Ringgold was born in 1930 in Harlem, a part of New York City. She had asthma as a child and was often too sick to go to school. To keep her daughter from getting bored, Willi Posey Jones, Faith's mother, taught her needlework and gave her fabric and needles and thread. Faith hated being sick, but she loved working with her hands and using her imagination to create beautiful things. So without realizing it Faith's mother helped her to become an artist.

Faith's mother and her father, Andrew, did something else that helped Faith achieve her goals— they helped her believe that she could accomplish whatever she set out to do. Faith's mother took her to see famous "stars," musicians such as Benny Goodman, Duke Ellington, and Judy Garland. Faith believed that she too would become a star—someday.

After she graduated from high school in 1948, Ringgold studied at the City College of New York to become an art teacher. That way she could support herself and do her creative work in her spare time. Ringgold taught students from kindergarten through college in the New York City public schools for almost twenty years. She painted when she could— landscapes at first and later on subjects having to do with the struggles of African Americans.

Teaching was hard work, but it helped her art to grow and change. She learned to use many materials by first having her students work with them. For a while, Ringgold taught at a high school where there was little money for art supplies, but a huge supply of dixie mesh, which is used for needlepoint. Ringgold used the mesh and taught her students complicated needle-work and bead weaving. She and her students talked and sometimes ate snacks while they worked. Ringgold explained, "The girls liked it, but the boys *loved* it."

Once, while Ringgold was teaching an African arts class, a student who had just seen an exhibition of

Aunt Edith, 1974, Aunt Bessie, 1974, Martin Luther King, 1975

Faith's watercolor paintings questioned her. She didn't understand why Ringgold, who loved to teach her students how to work with beads and fabric, never used these materials in her own art.

Ringgold didn't like being questioned, but she knew her student was right. She realized she was ignoring not only her childhood experiences, but also her interest in Africa and her heritage as a woman and an African American. In her family, women had worked with cloth for generations. Ringgold had learned needlework from her mother, and her mother had learned from Ringgold's great-grandmother, who had boiled and bleached flour sacks until they were pure white to use as quilt linings. Ringgold's great-great-grandmother, a slave, had also sewed quilts as part of her duties for a plantation owner.

Ringgold wondered what people would think if she used a needle and thread instead of paint and a paintbrush in her work. These were not the materials artists usually used. It was hard enough being an African American woman artist, without trying something new!

An exhibition of tankas, Tibetan paintings mounted on cloth, gave Ringgold the courage to change. Now her art really blossomed. She found that with cloth she could combine her interests in African art and her experiences growing up in Harlem. She left teaching and began sewing her own tankas and masks, sometimes with her mother's help.

Aunt Edith and *Aunt Bessie* are two life-size cloth masks. They are portraits of Faith's aunts. Because Edith was blind and depended on Bessie, the two masks are often shown together. They can be worn, much the way a costume is worn, but can also be hung from the ceiling or wall. The heads are painted canvas and the dresses are beaded, fringed, and embroidered cloth. The mouths of the aunts are open to show the need for women to speak out. One of the aunts wears a whistle to get attention.

Martin Luther King is another mask that Ringgold made. She made him larger than life-size because he was such an important person. King's head is made of foam rubber which Faith stitched and painted. The King mask looks very real.

Tar Beach, 1988

Ringgold began making quilts. One of them is *Sonny's Quilt,* after her friend Sonny Rollins, a well-known jazz musician. (It's shown on page sixty.) She remembers him always looking for an out-of-the-way spot to practice his horn so that he wouldn't disturb anyone. His favorite place was on the walkway of a bridge in New York. With paint and pieces of cloth, some tie-dyed like African fabric, Ringgold's quilt celebrates Rollins's work as an artist.

After a time, Ringgold began to write stories on her quilts. She had learned the art of storytelling from her mother, who was an expert. Family and neighbors would gather to hear Willi Posey Jones tell tales of past experiences and future dreams.

Tar Beach is one of Ringgold's story quilts. It is a large painting on cloth, surrounded by colorful pieces of quilted fabric. The story is written in the top and bottom borders. It is about a girl who is lying on a mattress on the roof of a building. Her family is having a picnic dinner there. As the girl watches the stars, she dreams of flying above the buildings and bridges. She tells her little brother, "Anyone can fly. All you need is somewhere to go that you can't get to any other way."

An editor at a publishing company saw *Tar Beach*. She thought the story quilt should be made into a children's book. Faith was eager to try. She made a lot of new paintings to go with the story, and the book was made. Now Faith is an author as well as an artist.

Ringgold has come a long way since she was a young girl at home with asthma. She has struggled to be accepted as an African American woman artist. She has tried to find her own voice in her art. She says, "I don't believe in not seeing the negative. But you can take that negative and make it positive." And that is exactly what Faith Ringgold did. Through her life and her art, she helps us realize that with hard work we can make our lives what we want.

THINKING ABOUT IT

1 Of all the works of art by Faith Ringgold shown in this article, which is your favorite? What do you like about it?

2 Carmen Lomas Garza writes about herself in *Family Pictures*. In the article about Faith Ringgold, someone else tells the story. How might the article be different if Ringgold were to write about herself?

3 You are in an art class taught by Faith Ringgold. She is teaching you how to use cloth, needles, beads, paint, and many other kinds of materials. What will you make? What materials will you use?

PAD and PENCIL

by David McCord

I drew a rabbit. John erased him
and not the dog I said had chased him.

I drew a bear on another page,
but John said, "Put him in a cage."

I drew some mice. John drew the cat
with nasty claws. The mice saw that.

I got them off the page real fast:
the things I draw don't *ever* last.

We drew a bird with one big wing:
he couldn't fly worth anything,

but sat there crumpled on a limb.
John's pencil did a job on *him*.

Three bats were next. I made them fly.
John smudged one out against the sky

above an owl he said could hoot.
He helped me with my wolf. The brute

had lots too long a tail, but we
concealed it all behind a tree.

By then I couldn't think of much
except to draw a rabbit hutch;

but since we had no rabbit now
I drew what must have been a cow,

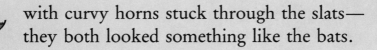

with curvy horns stuck through the slats—
they both looked something like the bats.

And feeling sad about the bear
inside his cage, I saw just where

I'd draw the door to let him out.
And that's just all of it, about.

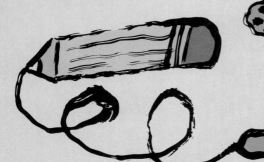

The BOLL WEEVIL

Verses selected and illustrated by

GLEN ROUNDS

The Boll Weevil is a mean little bug—
　　Came from Mexico, they say.
Came all the way to Texas, just looking for a place
　　to stay.
Just looking for a home, yes, looking for a home.

The first time I saw little Weevil
　　He was on the Western Plain.

Next time I saw the Weevil he was riding a Memphis
   train.
He was looking for a home, just looking for a home.

When the Farmer saw those Boll Weevils
They were in his rocking chair.
The next time they were in his corn field and they had
   all their family there,
Just fixing up a home, yes, fixing up a home.

The Boll Weevil say to the Farmer,
    "You can ride in that Ford machine,
But when I get through with your cotton you can't
    buy gasoline.
You won't have no home, won't have no home."

Oh, the Boll Weevil said to the Doctor,
    "Better pour out all your pills.
When I get through with the Farmer he cain't pay no
    doctor's bills.
He'll have no home, he'll have no home."

The Farmer say to the Woman,
  "What do you think of that?
Those devilish Boll Weevils have been eating my
  Stetson hat.
It's full of holes, it's full of holes."

The Merchant said to the Farmer,
  "Well, what do you think of that?
If you'll get rid of the Weevil I'll give you a brand
  new Stetson hat.
He's looking for a home, just looking for a home."

The Farmer took little Weevil
  And put him in Paris Green.
The Weevil said to the Farmer, "It's the best I've
  ever seen.
I'm goin' to have a home, a happy home."

The Farmer took the Boll Weevil
  And put him in a frying pan.
Weevil said to the Farmer, "It's mighty warm, but I'll
  stand it like a man.
This will be my home, yes, this will be my home."

The Weevil grabbed the Farmer
   And throwed him in the sand—
Put on the Farmer's overcoat and stood up like a
   natural man.
Said, "I'm going to have a home, a happy home."

The Boll Weevil said to the Farmer,
   "You better leave me alone.
I done et up all your cotton, now I'm starting on
   your corn.
I'll have a home, yes, I'll have a home."

The Farmer said to the Merchant,
   "I need some meat and meal."
"Get away from here, you son of a gun, you got Boll
   Weevils in your field.

Going to get your home, going to get your home."

The Farmer said to the Merchant,
"I didn't make but one bale,
But before I let you have that one I'll suffer and die
    in jail—
I'll have a home, I'll have a home!"

Well, the Merchant got half the cotton,
    The Boll Weevils got the rest.
Didn't leave the poor Farmer's wife but one old
    cotton dress,

And it's full of holes, all full of holes.

The Farmer said to the Banker,
    "We're in an awful fix.
The Boll Weevil et all our cotton up and left us
    only sticks.
We've got no home, we've got no home."

The Banker was bad as the Weevils,
    Said, "There's nothing I can do.
I can't lend you any more money for the Weevils
    might eat that too,
And leave it full of holes, all full of holes."

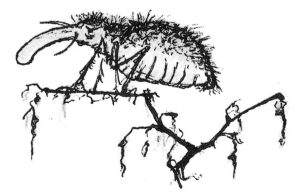

The Farmer said, "Come on, Old Woman,
    And we'll travel out West.
The Weevils et up everything we've got but this old
    cotton vest,
And it's full of holes, all full of holes."

Now if anyone should ask you
    Who it was that wrote this here song,
You can say it was just a homeless Farmer with ragged
    britches on,
Just hunting for a home, yes, hunting for a home.

THE BOLL WEEVIL

Arranged by Patty Zeitlin

THE BOLL WEEVIL IS A MEAN LIT-TLE BUG CAME FROM MEX-I-CO THEY

SAY. CAME ALL THE WAY FROM TEX-AS, JUST LOOK-ING FOR A PLACE TO

STAY JUST LOOK-ING FOR A HOME JUST LOOK-ING FOR A HOME

Music from the singing of Jake Zeitlin as he learned it from Carl Sandburg in the early 1920s.

E·79

The Traveling Sign Painters

by Glen Rounds

Not many people remember the sign painters who traveled from town to town in the old days, refurbishing old signs or painting new ones.

The sign painters in that day, like the scouts, trappers, keelboatmen, loggers, and locomotive drivers of the time, were a special breed of men. They had been everywhere and seen everything worth seeing. At least most of them claimed to have done so—which amounts to practically the same thing.

They traveled north and south and east and west across the country and, wherever they went, the people of the small towns welcomed them as eagerly as they did the dog and pony shows, the tent revivalist, or the chautauqua.

To watch such a man take a piece of chalk and casually sketch in the letters of a sign on the shining glass of a storefront was a magical thing, well worth seeing.

And when, after making a small change in the outline of a letter here or there, he

E·81

Stroke by stroke the outlines of the letters appeared, one after the other, as if by magic. The straight lines were straight and bold, the curves fat and round, and the points sharp and sure.

It was truly a thing to see.

opened his battered box and began searching among the small cans of paint, the crowd would press close to watch his every movement.

And by the time he'd dipped a brush into the paint and was drawing it back and forth on a scrap of cardboard to flatten the bristles, most of the storekeepers up and down the street had probably come out to join the watchers.

Then, when he was sure that every eye was on him, he faced the glass and in one firm, sure stroke drew a line from top to bottom of the first letter, flicking the brush out to the left at the last moment in a neat, sweeping curve.

But, best of all, while giving the people this glimpse into the magical world of art, the sign painter both entertained and informed them by sharing with them his vast knowledge of the world.

As he worked, and during the times he took for a little rest, or to select another brush, he would describe great cities like Amarillo, San Antone', Kansas City, and a hundred others in such detail that his listeners could almost see the streets and houses. He knew where all the railroads ran, and could give eyewitness accounts of great floods, fires, train wrecks, and other catastrophes the listeners had only read about in the papers.

At one time there were hundreds of these fellows drifting about the country— all of them splendid craftsmen and master storytellers. But probably the best known of them all was my old friend, Mr. Xenon Zebulon Yowder. He spoke of himself as being the "World's Bestest and Fastest Sign Painter," and perhaps he was.

Our trails crossed now and again in Missouri, Kansas, Texas, or the Dakotas—and at various times we even traveled and worked together. So I heard at first hand the details of dozens of the fantastic things he'd done. A lesser man would have been accused of stretching the truth, or even downright prevarication. But Mr. Yowder's very appearance inspired belief. And with the possible exception of a few harmless embellishments here and there, I think his tales were probably very, very close to the exact truth, in all respects.

He was simply a man who, in his spare time, did seemingly impossible things as regularly and easily as ordinary men tie their shoelaces in the mornings.

Mr. Yowder
and the
Train Robbers

WRITTEN AND ILLUSTRATED BY
GLEN ROUNDS

Mr. Xenon Zebulon Yowder's famous adventure with the gang of train robbers happened many, many years ago when the country was, in some respects, wilder, than it is now—and train robbery much more common.

But over the years, through many tellings and retellings, the story has become garbled beyond recognition. There are folk who are firmly convinced that Mr. Yowder was himself a member of the gang. And there are others just as firmly convinced that, instead, Mr. Yowder faced the desperados in a shoot-out, and single-handedly laid them all low.

The truth, however, as so often happens, lies somewhere in between. And here, for the first time, is the true and unadorned account of what actually did occur—how the adventure came about, and how it ended, as well as a detailed description of the part the twenty-seven rattlesnakes played in the affair.

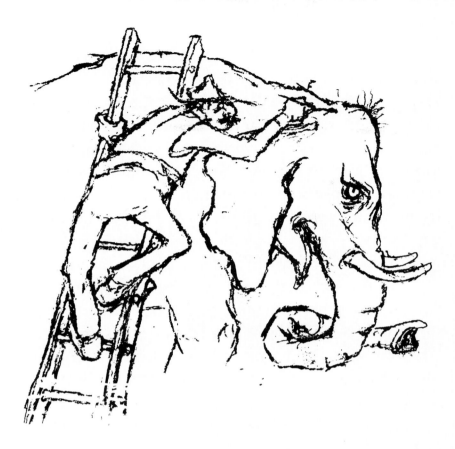

Mr. Yowder, who claimed to be "The World's Bestest and Fastest Sign Painter," would probably never have gotten involved with the train robber gang if it hadn't been for his meeting with Mr. Pernell P. Hagadorn.

Mr. Hagadorn was not a train robber nor, as far as anyone knows, did he even know any such. At the time we speak of he owned an overall factory, making overalls that were said to wear like elephant hide. And he wanted Mr. Yowder to paint life-sized elephants on the sides of barns and stores across the state of Kansas to advertise his product.

But Mr. Yowder liked variety in his work—
something different every day—so he told Mr.
Hagadorn that the idea of spending the summer painting the same sign over and over didn't appeal to him.

Mr. Hagadorn, however, said that to make the
job more interesting, Mr. Yowder could change the
elephant's expression from time to time, or have him
facing in different directions. And, besides, he would
pay him very well.

So in the end Mr. Yowder agreed to take the job.

All through that summer he painted elephants
day after day, no two alike. Some looked fierce and
some looked kindly, some faced east and some faced
west, but all were magnificent beasts, and were much
admired by passing farmers and tourists for years
afterwards.

By the middle of August there wasn't a store or
barn anywhere in Kansas that didn't have an elephant
painted on it. And when Mr. Hagadorn paid Mr.
Yowder off, he was so pleased with the job that he
gave him a few dollars extra as a bonus.

With all that money in his pocket, Mr. Yowder
thought he would take a little vacation to sort of rest
up from painting elephants all summer. The lady who
ran the boardinghouse told him there was good fishing
back in the hills south of town. So right after supper,
Mr. Yowder, who purely loved to fish, hurried across
the street to the hardware store and bought himself a
fish pole and some hooks. And next morning he rode
out a few miles on a rancher's wagon and dropped off
where a clear stream crossed the road.

The stream ran through some of the roughest country Mr. Yowder had ever seen, but by noon he had caught a nice mess of fish. So he built a fire in a little clearing and cooked some of the smaller ones for his dinner.

After he'd eaten, Mr. Yowder lay back on the soft grass and took himself a nap. When he woke it was well along in the afternoon, so he gathered up his things and started looking about for a shortcut back to the main road.

But he had gone only a little distance when, coming out from between two low hills, he found

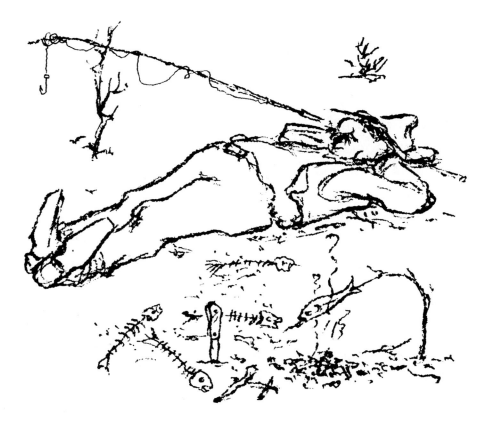

himself at the head of a weed-grown street running
between the tumbledown buildings of a
long-abandoned settlement.

The old-fashioned false fronts leaned at crazy
angles and there were great holes in most of the
sagging roofs and porches. But when he was over his
first surprise, Mr. Yowder cautiously explored the
nearest buildings. He found a few rusting cans, and
the usual litter of old magazines and papers, but
otherwise there was no sign that anyone had visited
the place for years.

The sign across the front of the old hotel had not
entirely weathered away, and the roof over what had
been the lobby didn't seem to leak too badly. So Mr.

Yowder decided it would be a good place to camp for a few days while he caught up on his fishing. The only well he'd found had no water in it, just some trash and the rickety ladder the long-forgotten well digger hadn't bothered to pull out of the hole when he abandoned the job. But Mr. Yowder figured he could carry what water he needed from the creek.

So, dragging a broken chair out onto the porch, he sat a while, admiring the view before starting back to the boardinghouse and supper.

Next morning when he rode out of town with the mail carrier, Mr. Yowder was carrying a couple of blankets, a frying pan, and several days' supply of coffee, bacon, and some canned goods stuffed into a grain sack.

Back at the abandoned town, he swept out the lobby of the old hotel, arranged his plunder, and checked to see that the rusty stove was in working order. Then he dug a can of worms and hurried to the creek.

When he came back around noon with another nice mess of fish, the biggest rattlesnake he'd ever seen was sunning himself on the hotel porch.

The snake started down through a hole in the porch floor, but Mr. Yowder spoke to him in Snake— you probably remember that Mr. Yowder had learned to speak Snake down in Oklahoma some years before—and asked him to wait up a minute.

As might be expected, the rattlesnake was somewhat surprised at hearing his language spoken. But he waited politely while Mr. Yowder explained that he just wanted to camp in the building for a few days, and would try to be as little trouble as possible.

The snake said it had been a long time since he'd had anyone to talk to, or had heard any news, and that Mr. Yowder was welcome to stay around as long as he liked.

So Mr. Yowder dragged a chair out onto the porch and read the snake the more interesting bits from a newspaper he happened to have in his pocket. Between items the snake told Mr. Yowder about his sleeping place under the building, and of the small happenings in the town.

It was sundown almost before they knew it, and Mr. Yowder asked the snake to stay and have a bite of supper with him.

The snake thanked him, but said he had a broken fang that made his mouth so sore he couldn't eat. However, he would take a small saucer of cold coffee and condensed milk, if it wasn't too much trouble.

But Mr. Yowder had done considerable simple dentistry and, after asking the snake to open wide, he quickly smoothed and rounded the jagged end of the broken fang with the little file he carried in his pocket for sharpening fishhooks.

When he'd finished, the snake ran his tongue over the place and said it felt as good as new, and maybe he would have a little supper after all.

The weather stayed fine, and Mr. Yowder went fishing every morning, but in the afternoons he and the snake talked or took naps on the sunny porch. One day when the wind was blowing scraps of paper across the porch floor, the snake found what he thought must be a picture of one of his skinny relatives.

Mr. Yowder explained that the paper was a page from an old Boy Scout handbook, and the picture was simply a diagram showing how to tie a square knot. Not having any string or rope handy, he took the snake's tail in one hand, and his neck in the other and loosely tied them together to show how it was done.

The old rattlesnake was very pleased with the trick, and practiced tying and untying the knot himself. At first, as most people do, he sometimes ended up with a slipknot instead, but before long he was able to tie it right every time.

Later he invented a sort of game. After tying himself into a loop he'd roll down the street hoopsnake fashion. Said it was the most fun he'd had in years!

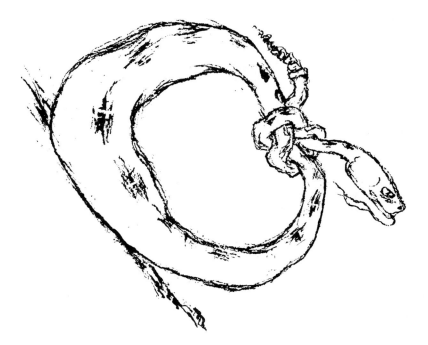

Then one evening when Mr. Yowder and the old snake were inside fixing an early supper, four strangers rode up to the end of the street and stopped their horses.

They were dangerous-looking men, unshaven and with pistols in their belts and rifles in saddle scabbards.

"This is the hideout I told you about," the leader said. "Nobody's been here for years. We'll rob the train at Alkali Springs tomorrow, and come back here for a day or two while we rest and divide the loot. The sheriff will never think of looking for us here."

Then one of the riders behind him pointed to the smoke coming out of the old hotel chimney. "Somebody's already found the hideout," he said. "Let's get out of here!"

The leader looked again. "I don't see any sign of

horses," he said after a little. "It may just be some old prospector or some such. Let's take a look."

So, with their hands on their guns, they rode cautiously up to the edge of the old porch.

When he heard the horses, Mr. Yowder looked out through the broken window, then turned to the snake and said, "You'd better get out of sight. I don't like the looks of those jaspers."

When the old rattlesnake had slithered down through a hole in the floor, Mr. Yowder stepped outside and told the strangers "Howdy."

The leader explained to Mr. Yowder that they were stock buyers just passing through the country, and wondered if they could stay the night.

Even though they didn't look like stock buyers to him, Mr. Yowder told the men they were welcome, and suggested that they camp down by the creek where there was water for their horses.

But the leader dismounted and pushed rudely past Mr. Yowder, looked around, then remarked that since Mr. Yowder was all alone, they'd just throw their beds down inside and keep him company.

"It's all right," the leader told the others when he went outside. "The old man is alone, so we'll keep close watch on him tonight and figure what to do with him in the morning."

Mr. Yowder was sure he'd seen pictures of the strangers on reward posters somewhere, and figured that as soon as they went to sleep, he'd sneak out and go for the sheriff. But the men kept the lantern burning all night, and every time Mr. Yowder stirred, he found one or another of them awake and watching him.

In the morning the strangers were up early, and the one that went out to bring up the horses told the leader about the old well outside. "That's just the place for you, old man," the leader said to Mr. Yowder. "We've got to rob a train today, and we'd like to be sure you'll be right here when we come back tonight."

So they made Mr. Yowder climb down into the well, and when he was on the bottom, they pulled the ladder up and threw it on the ground.

Mr. Yowder listened to the robbers ride away, then sat down (there wasn't room for him to pace around) and wondered what would become of him.

It was well after sunup when some pebbles rattled down from above and he found the old snake looking over the edge of the well. The snake hissed something but, as all snakes do, he had a very soft voice and Mr. Yowder couldn't make out what he was saying even when he'd repeated it. So, after nodding a couple of times, the snake pulled his head back and disappeared.

Then Mr. Yowder felt lonelier than ever.

He knew there was no way the snake could help him out of his predicament, but it would have been

nice if he'd have stayed around just to look over the edge now and again.

All forenoon he sat there while the sunlight crept slowly down the wall. Noon came, with the sun shining straight down to the bottom of the well, but still there was no sign of his only friend, the old rattlesnake.

Mr. Yowder grew more and more discouraged.

But sometime late in the afternoon, Mr. Yowder began hearing small scufflings and hissings from above.

This went on for some time, then some bits of dirt fell on his hat. Looking up he saw the head of a strange rattlesnake slowly coming into sight at the top of the well. When half his body was in sight, the

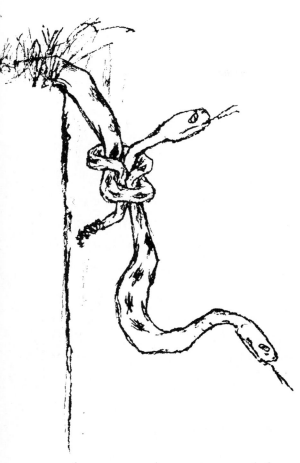

snake stopped moving and for a while simply hung
head downwards against the wall.

After some more small noises from somewhere
out of sight, the strange snake again started moving
downwards, inch by inch. Then the head of another
strange snake appeared behind the first. Mr. Yowder
could scarcely believe his eyes when he saw that the
two were tied together, neck to tail, in a perfect
square knot!

There were many delays, but one after another,
snake after snake wriggled into sight—each one's neck
tied to the tail of the one ahead.

Before long the knotted rope of well-muscled rattlesnakes hung nearly to the bottom of the well. The nearest snake, seeing that he was easily within Mr. Yowder's reach, hissed to the one above, "Far enough! Pass it on."

From snake to snake the word was passed upwards to the ones out of sight at the top.

And after short delay word from somewhere above was passed back down again, "Tell him to climb up."

Taking a firm hold of the nearest snake's body, Mr. Yowder tugged a couple of times to make sure the line was securely anchored. Then, spitting on his hands, he climbed up hand over hand, and soon scrambled safely out on top.

Mr. Yowder found the old rattlesnake tied to the end of the line, with his tail wrapped several times around a nearby post. Telling him to hang on just a minute more, Mr. Yowder quickly pulled the others back out of the well, coiling them neatly on the grass as he did so.

His weight had pulled the knots so tight the snakes were unable to undo them, and it took Mr. Yowder a half hour or more to get them untied from one another.

When the snakes had finished stretching the kinks out of their necks and tails, Mr. Yowder invited them all up to the hotel for cold coffee and condensed milk. There was plenty of coffee left in the pot the robbers had made for their breakfast, and he found several unopened cans of condensed milk among their supplies.

The snakes waited politely while Mr. Yowder
filled some old saucers and set them on the floor, but
when he waved a hand and said "Drink up!" they
didn't hesitate. Three or four to the saucer, they began
thirstily lapping up milk and coffee.

While the snakes were busy with their snacks,
Mr. Yowder—being careful not to step on their tails—
paced up and down the room, thinking.

When everyone was finished he told them all how
much he appreciated their help in getting him out of
the well.

The old rattlesnake said it wasn't anything, really. He'd simply happened to think of the square-knot trick and passed the word among his neighbors.

Then Mr. Yowder went on to say there most surely would be a large reward offered for the train robbers, and he'd figured out a way to capture them, if the snakes were willing to help him one more time.

After he had carefully explained his plan, the snakes talked it over among themselves, then said they'd be right pleased to help him out. It was years since anything exciting had happened in the neighborhood, and catching a band of robbers would make an even better story than their pulling Mr. Yowder out of the well. They'd probably even get their pictures in the paper.

Then a snake they called Joe spoke up and said that he'd purely like to help capture the robbers, but he thought he'd strained his back that afternoon. Mr. Yowder said not to worry, the other snakes could handle the job without trouble, and for Joe to go along home and take it easy for a day or two.

By that time it was beginning to get dark, and they heard the robbers' horses outside. The snakes disappeared through holes in the floor, and Mr. Yowder hid himself in a little closet under the old stairs just as the robbers stomped in, dragging several heavy mailbags, and an iron Wells Fargo chest.

They seemed to be in fine spirits, and from their loud talk, Mr. Yowder discovered that after they'd held up the train, they had robbed the passengers as well as the mail car.

The leader lit the lantern and emptied one of the sacks on the table. "We'll count the express car money later," he said. "But first let's see what we got off the passengers."

As soon as the robbers were busy sorting through the pile of loot, trying on diamond rings, selecting gold watches and watch chains and fancy stickpins, Mr. Yowder signaled the snakes by tapping twice, softly, on the floor with his boot heel.

The robbers were so busy with their loot they didn't notice the soft scaly rustlings as the rattlesnakes

came up through the holes in the old floor and gathered in a circle around the table.

When they were all in their places, Mr. Yowder stepped quietly out of the closet and said, "Don't move, gents, until you've taken a good look at what's down by your feet."

They did as he said, and saw big rattlesnakes in the patches of lamplight while beady eyes and white fangs glittered in the shadows around their feet. And then, to add to their fright, the terrible buzzing of twenty-six sets of rattles suddenly filled the room.

One robber fainted but another caught him
before he could fall down among the snakes.

When the sun came up, Mr. Yowder yawned and
said, "Well, let's go to town and see the sheriff."

He told two of the unhappy robbers to each take
a handle of the Wells Fargo chest while the others
carried the heavy canvas bags. Then with rattlesnakes
crawling in front, on either side, and behind them,
they stumbled along the old road.

The robber leader complained that his feet hurt,
and asked if they couldn't ride their horses. But Mr.

Yowder told him that walking was fine exercise and, besides, they'd have no use for horses where they were going.

By the time they climbed the last rocky hill and came out onto the main road, the complaining robbers were footsore and out of breath, so Mr. Yowder let them stop for a little rest.

After making sure the circle of snakes was carefully guarding them, he looked towards the town and noticed a high, fast-moving cloud of dust rapidly moving his way. As it came closer he saw under it a big posse of mounted men riding at a gallop behind the sheriff, whose white hat and gold badge glittered in the sun.

Telling the rattlesnakes and the robbers to stay where they were, Mr. Yowder—with a big smile on his face—stepped out into the middle of the road and held up his hand.

But the posse neither slowed nor stopped. As they came nearer, the sound of the horses' hooves drowned out the fierce buzzing of the rattlesnakes, and at the last minute Mr. Yowder had to dive for the ditch to avoid being ridden down.

As he thundered past on his foam-flecked horse, the sheriff hollered, "Can't stop now. We're looking for the train robbers! THERE'S A BIG REWARD!"

After the posse had passed and the thick cloud of dust had finally settled, Mr. Yowder looked around and found himself alone.

To save themselves from being trampled by the horses, the rattlesnakes had scattered into the high grass, for which Mr. Yowder could not really blame them. And finding themselves unguarded, the train

robbers had snatched up their loot and scuttled back into the thick brush at the bottom of the rocky slope.

There was no way Mr. Yowder could catch them again, so after a while he dusted himself off and walked on into town. When he got there the Denver train was just pulling in, so he bought himself a ticket and climbed aboard.

He often wondered, in years afterwards, if the robbers were ever caught, and if they were, who got the reward he so nearly collected.

And that is the TRUE STORY of Mr. Yowder's adventure with the train robber gang.

Thinking About It

1. *The boll weevils and the rattlesnakes that can tie themselves into square knots come to your school. Hundreds of them pour in the door of your classroom. What do you do?*

2. *Compare "The Boll Weevil" to* Mr. Yowder and the Train Robbers. *Are the song and story similar in any way? Look at the pictures. In what way are the illustrations in the two pieces similar?*

3. *Create your own helpful or harmful animal and tell a story about it as Glen Rounds did in "The Boll Weevil" and* Mr. Yowder and the Train Robbers.

Another Book by Glen Rounds

Mr. Yowder and the Windwagon. *Regular covered wagons are too slow for Mr. Yowder. If ships can use wind to sail across the ocean, he reasons, why can't wagons use wind to sail across the prairie?*

ROXABOXEN

Marian called it Roxaboxen.
(She always knew the name of everything.)
There across the road, it looked like any rocky hill—
nothing but sand and rocks, some old wooden boxes,
cactus and greasewood and thorny ocotillo—
but it was a special place.

ILLUSTRATIONS BY
BARBARA COONEY

The street between Roxaboxen and the houses curved
    like a river,
so Marian named it the River Rhode.
After that you had to ford a river to reach Roxaboxen.

Of course all of Marian's sisters came:
Anna May and Frances and little Jean.
Charles from next door, even though he was twelve.
Oh, and Eleanor, naturally,
and Jamie with his brother Paul.
Later on there were others, but these were the first.
Well, not really the first.
Roxaboxen had always been there
and must have belonged to others, long before.

When Marian dug up a tin box filled with round
    black pebbles
everyone knew what it was: it was a buried treasure.
Those pebbles were the money of Roxaboxen.
You could still find others like them if you looked
    hard enough.
So some days became treasure-hunting days, with
    everybody trying to find that special kind.
And then on other days you might just find one
    without even looking.

A town of Roxaboxen began to grow, traced in lines
    of stone:
Main Street first, edged with the whitest ones,
and then the houses.
Charles made his of the biggest stones.
After all, he was the oldest.

At first the houses were very plain, but soon they all
 began to add more rooms.
The old wooden boxes could be shelves or tables or
 anything you wanted.
You could find pieces of pottery for dishes.
Round pieces were best.

Later on there was a town hall.
Marian was mayor, of course;
that was just the way she was.
Nobody minded.

After a while they added other streets.
Frances moved to one of them and built herself a new
 house outlined in desert glass,
bits of amber, amethyst, and sea-green:
a house of jewels.

And because everybody had plenty of money,
there were plenty of shops.
Jean helped Anna May in the bakery—
pies and cakes and bread baked warm in the sun.
There were two ice cream parlors.
Was Paul's ice cream the best, or Eleanor's?
Everybody kept trying them both.
(In Roxaboxen you can eat all the ice cream you want.)

Everybody had a car.
All you needed was something round for a
    steering wheel.
Of course, if you broke the speed limit you had to go
    to jail.
The jail had cactus on the floor to make it
    uncomfortable,
and Jamie was the policeman.
Anna May, quiet little Anna May, was always
    speeding—
you'd think she liked to go to jail.

But ah, if you had a horse, you could go as fast as
    the wind.
There were no speed limits for horses,
and you didn't have to stay on the roads.
All you needed for a horse was a stick and some kind
    of bridle,
and you could gallop anywhere.

Sometimes there were wars.

Once there was a great war, boys against girls.

Charles and Marian were the generals.

The girls had Fort Irene, and they were all girl scouts.

The boys made a fort at the other end of Roxaboxen,
 and they were all bandits.

Oh, the raids were fierce, loud with whooping and the
   stamping of horses!
The whirling swords of ocotillo had sharp thorns—
but when you reached your fort you were safe.

E·118

Roxaboxen had a cemetery, in case anyone died,
but the only grave in it was for a dead lizard.
Each year when the cactus bloomed, they decorated
    the grave with flowers.

Sometimes in the winter, when everybody was at
    school and the weather was bad,
no one went to Roxaboxen at all, not for weeks
    and weeks.
But it didn't matter;
Roxaboxen was always waiting.
Roxaboxen was always there.
And spring came, and the ocotillo blossomed,
and everybody sucked the honey from its flowers,
and everybody built new rooms, and everybody
    decided to have jeweled windows.
That summer there were three new houses on the
    east slope
and two new shops on Main Street.

And so it went.
The seasons changed, and the years went by.
Roxaboxen was always there.

The years went by, and the seasons changed,
until at last the friends had all grown tall,
and one by one, they moved away
to other houses, to other towns.
So you might think that was the end of Roxaboxen—
but oh, no.

Because none of them ever forgot Roxaboxen.
Not one of them ever forgot.
Years later, Marian's children listened to stories of that
    place
and fell asleep dreaming dreams of Roxaboxen.
Gray-haired Charles picked up a black pebble on
    the beach
and stood holding it,
remembering Roxaboxen.

More than fifty years later, Frances went back
and Roxaboxen was still there.
She could see the white stones bordering Main Street,
and there where she had built her house
the desert glass still glowed—
amethyst, amber, and sea-green.

THINKING
ABOUT IT

1. You say *Roxaboxen* to someone who has been there. What does that person tell you about the place? When you show that person a picture from the story, what does the person say?

2. If you visited Roxaboxen, what would you explore? Show what you'd do if you were in one of the pictures. Reread parts of the story for ideas.

3. The children in Roxaboxen invented their own town. Now it is your turn to make up a special place of your own. What will your town be called? Who will live there? What will you do for fun?

My Dress Is Old

My dress is old, but at night the moon is
   kind.
Then I wear a beautiful moon-colored dress.

Tribe Unknown

I Watched an Eagle Soar

Grandmother,
I watched an eagle soar
high in the sky
until a cloud covered him up.
Grandmother,
I still saw the eagle
behind my eyes.

Virginia Driving Hawk Sneve

Three Wondrous Buildings

BY PHILIP M. ISAACSON

This is a building in a small city in northern India (1). People come from all over the world to see it. Many of them come because they feel that it is the most beautiful building in the world. It is called the Taj Mahal and it is a valentine from a great emperor to a wife who died when she was very young. It is made of marble the color of cream. Each afternoon the sun changes the color of the Taj Mahal. First it turns it pink, then yellow, then the color of apricots. In the evening it becomes brown, and when the moon shines on it, it is blue and gray. In the moonlight it becomes the old emperor, asleep and dreaming.

The Taj Mahal is about three hundred years old. This building is much older (2). It was built about 2,500 years ago and stands on a white marble hill in Greece. Because it too is made of white marble, it seems to grow out of that hill as though it were a

1.

2.

group of great trees standing in a small forest. It is called the Parthenon in honor of an ancient Greek goddess. Though it is made only of marble posts—called columns—and a very simple roof, it is just as famous as the Taj Mahal (3) and has just as many admirers. Many people feel that it is the most beautiful building in the world.

This building is also very famous (4). It is in a French city near Paris called Chartres. Its name is Our Lady of Chartres. One part of it is almost nine hundred years old and so it is older than the Taj Mahal but not nearly as old as the Parthenon. It is made of a hard stone that is not very friendly and has many moods. On a sunny day, with fast-moving clouds behind it, Chartres looks like a great ship

3.

sailing along against the sky, but on a dark day it can be cold and gray and a little frightening. Chartres is another building that many people feel is the most beautiful of all.

In many ways these buildings are alike. All of them are places of worship: the Taj Mahal is a mosque, the Parthenon is a temple, Chartres is a church. Each was built in honor of a woman; the Taj Mahal honors a young wife, the Parthenon honors a young goddess, Chartres honors a saint. Finally, all three are very beautiful.

In other ways, however, they're not alike at all. The Taj Mahal sits in a riverside garden with pools of water to reflect its soft shapes. The Parthenon is short and as powerful as a king on a mountain throne.

Chartres is hard and sharp with towers tall enough to slice open the sky—towers so tall that you can see them from afar, long before you see the great cathedral beneath them.

These wonderful buildings tell us many things about beauty. First they tell us that there are many kinds of beauty. There is beauty in buildings that look soft and creamy, in buildings that look short and strong, and in buildings that are sharp and tall. They also tell us that all beautiful buildings, indeed all beautiful things, have a magical feeling about them. That feeling is called harmony. A building has harmony when everything about it—its shape, its walls, its windows and doors—seems just right. Each must be a perfect companion for the other. When each suits the other so well that they come to belong to one another, the building is a work of art. The person who plans such a building—who designs it—is an artist, sometimes a very great artist.

4.

Buildings Are Restless

by Philip M. Isaacson

Buildings are restless. They're always on the move, always changing. Each time we look at them they seem a little different.

Early in the morning they're washed with golden light. Late in the afternoon they reach out and catch long shadows. And at sunset they vanish, leaving black footprints against the sky to remind us of where they stood at dawn. In the winter they hide their roofs, their ledges, and porches under sheets of ice and snow. And in the summer they lurk behind trees and awnings and flowers. In the fall the last colors of the leaves

argue with them, but in the spring they stand alone. In the spring, trees are bare, lawns are asleep and buildings stand crisp and clear in the new air.

Buildings grow soft on hazy days and disappear when the haze turns to fog. On rainy days they stand on their heads in the puddles around them and, if they're near a river, they race upstream as quickly as the river flows by them. When they're being repaired, they often pull soft, silvery sheets over themselves. Some buildings twirl, some drill their way into the sky, and some bump the sky aside. Some—such as circus tents— move from town to town every day or so and some stand still but have parts that seem to move. Think of a building that has a dome and soon you'll discover that the dome is a great balloon that was a prisoner deep inside the building and is on its way to freedom.

Of course, buildings don't really hop around or vanish into the sky, but they do seem to move. Light, weather, the seasons, water, even trees change their looks and make them dance for us. I've seen buildings that sweep along the streets of a city, buildings that twirl on the sidewalks of New York, that slice the edges of the sky like a cavalry sword and race with the clouds.

And every building that I know—even my home— looks a little different to me each time I see it. It may grow taller or fatter; its color may seem deeper or faded. At times shadows wiggle across its face and as they do, my home wiggles a bit too.

Buildings have performed for me since I was a boy. I hope to write more about them in the future.

Pulling It All Together

1 Author Philip Isaacson describes the buildings in this selection as "wondrous." What wondrous buildings have you seen? What makes a building wondrous?

2 Carmen Lomas Garza has decided to paint some new paintings. She travels to visit Mr. Yowder. What will she paint? Next, she visits Roxaboxen. What will she decide to paint there?

3 Think of the characters you met in this book—Mr. Yowder, the Crow, Faith Ringgold, Frances, and all the others. Each one used his or her imagination. Choose two of the characters. Have them talk to each other about being in this book. What would they say to each other?

Whoppers, Tall Tales and Other Lies

by Alvin Schwartz
illustrations by Glen Rounds
Fantastic, outrageous lies
and stories that could never,
ever have possibly happened!

Marc Chagall

by Ernest Raboff
Chagall's bright, imaginative
paintings of everyday lives
are explained. Behind
each picture is a story of
happiness or love.

Edward Lear, King of Nonsense

by Gloria Kamen
Edward Lear loved to make
children laugh. His travels
led him to create nonsense
in his "Learical limericks"
and "nartist pigshers."

How I Hunted the Little Fellows

by Boris Zhitkov
illustrations by
Paul O. Zelinsky
A Russian boy's curiosity
takes over as he longs to
touch a mysterious,
forbidden, miniature
steamship. He knows it's
filled with little men that
only he can save.

There's a Rainbow in My Closet

by Patti Stren
No one understands Emma's
art! She paints what she feels
and draws what's real. But,
what's real to her isn't at all
real to her teacher. Emma
is caught between pleasing
her teacher and creating
her dreams.

How to Really Fool Yourself

by Vicki Cobb
Mirages and optical illusions mingle as dozens of stunts, sound effects, and mysteries are explained. See why you were fooled.

Home Place

by Crescent Dragonwagon
illustrations by Jerry Pinkney
A forgotten home site and spring daffodils help a family of hikers imagine the past owners' colorful lives.

Shadow Play

by Paul Fleischman
illustrations by Eric Beddows
Those who dare will open their eyes to giant shadows stalking the stage. Can you believe your eyes or your mind, watching the shadows creep into the show?

Autobiography

Family Pictures is an unusual sort of autobiography. Carmen Lomas Garza uses her paintings along with her stories to tell about special events in her life.

Biography

In the biography of Faith Ringgold, Faith's paintings tell almost as much about her as the words of the article do.

Character

Mr. Yowder is a very funny character made up by Glen Rounds. The old snake is another. One reason Mr. Yowder is funny is because he doesn't seem at all afraid of the snakes. The snakes are funny because they act like people. Part of the humor comes because the characters' reactions are so different from what we would expect from our experience.

Exaggeration

In *Mr. Yowder and the Train Robbers*, there are many examples of exaggeration, such as the signs that claim Hagadorn's overalls wear like elephant hide. Exaggeration adds to the humor of the story.

Fable

A **fable** is a short story, usually with animal characters, that gives a lesson at the end. "The Crow and the Pitcher" is a fable. Though "The Crow and the Pitcher" rhymes, most fables do not.

Stage Directions

Notice that a list of the characters as well as the time and setting appear at the beginning of the play "Mother Goose Gumshoe." At various points in the play, the playwright suggests things for the characters to do while they say their lines. For example *(Sit)* means that the character Mrs. H. Dumpty should sit in a chair on stage. These directions are called **stage directions.**

Tall Tale

The one thing that separates tall tales from all other kinds of folk tales is exaggeration. Babe, Paul Bunyan's blue ox, measures "forty-two axhandles between the eyes...." Pecos Bill lassoes the big dipper.

Vocabulary from your selections

am·a·teur (am′ə chər *or* am′ə tər), **1** a person who does something for pleasure, not for money: *Only amateurs can compete in college sports.* **2** of amateurs; by amateurs. **1** *noun,* **2** *adjective.*

a·non·y·mous (ə non′ə məs), by or from a person whose name is not known or given: *Hang up when you receive an anonymous call. adjective.*

au·di·tion (ô dish′ən), **1** a hearing to test the ability of a singer, actor, or other performer: *The auditions for the school play will be held Wednesday.* **2** to perform at or give such a hearing **1** *noun,* **2** *verb.*

boll weevil—about 1/5 inch long

boll weevil, a small beetle with a long snout whose larva is hatched in young cotton bolls and does great damage to them. *noun.*

bor·der (bôr′dər), **1** the side, edge, or boundary of anything, or the part near it. **2** to touch at the edge or boundary: *Canada borders on the U.S.* **3** a strip on the edge of anything for strength or ornament: *a lace border.* **1,3** *noun,* **2** *verb.*

cem·e·ter·y (sem′ə ter′ē), a place for burying the dead. *noun, plural* **cem·e·ter·ies.**

cli·ent (klī′ənt), a person for whom a lawyer, accountant, or other professional person acts. *noun.*

com·pan·ion (kəm pan′yən), one who often goes along with or accompanies another; one who shares in what another is doing.

com·pli·cat·ed (kom′plə kā′tid), **1** hard to understand. **2** made up of many parts; complex: *An automobile engine is a complicated machine. adjective.*

con·stel·la·tion (kon′stə lā′shən), a group of stars that forms a recognized pattern. There are 88 constellations in the sky. *noun.*

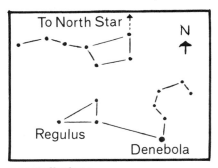

constellations

de·par·ture (di pär′chər), **1** the act of going away; act of leaving: *His departure was sudden.* **2** a turning away; change: *a departure from our old custom. noun.*

a	hat	i	it	oi	oil	ch	child	ə stands for:
ā	age	ī	ice	ou	out	ng	long	a in about
ä	far	o	hot	u	cup	sh	she	e in taken
e	let	ō	open	ù	put	th	thin	i in pencil
ē	equal	ô	order	ü	rule	ᴛʜ	then	o in lemon
ėr	term					zh	measure	u in circus

ev·i·dence (ev′ə dəns), facts; proof; anything that shows or makes clear: *The jam on his face was evidence that he had been in the kitchen. noun.*

fab·ric (fab′rik), a woven or knitted material; cloth. Velvet, denim, and linen are fabrics. *noun.*

fa·mous (fā′məs), very well known; noted. *adjective.*

fi·nal·ist (fī′nl ist), a person who has performed well enough to take part in the final round of an athletic or educational contest. *noun.*

flood (flud), **1** a great flow of water over what is usually dry land: *The heavy rains caused a serious flood near the river.* **2** to flow over; cover or fill with water. **1** *noun.* **2** *verb.*

ford (fôrd), **1** a place where a river, stream, or other body of water is not too deep to cross by walking through the water. **2** to cross a river, stream, or other body of water by walking or driving through the water: *We will have to ford the river below the falls.* **1** *noun,* **2** *verb.*

fraz·zled (fraz′əld), nervously tired or worn out. *adjective.*

hon·or (on′ər), **1** credit for acting well; glory or fame; good name: *It was greatly to her honor to be given a scholarship.* **2 honors,** special mention given to a student for having done work much above the average. **3** a source of credit; person or thing that reflects honor. **4** a sense of what is right or proper; nobility of mind. **5** great respect; high regard. **6** to show respect to. **1-5** *noun,* **6** *verb.*

in·di·cate (in′də kāt), **1** to point out; point to; show; make known: *The arrow on the sign indicates the way to go.* **2** to be a sign of: *Fever indicates illness. verb,* **in·di·cates, in·di·cat·ed, in·di·cat·ing.**

in·spire (in spīr′), **1** to fill with a thought or feeling: *A chance to try again inspired us with hope.* **2** to cause thought or feeling. **3** to fill with excitement. **4** to arouse effort or activity in someone. *verb,* **in·spires, in·spired, in·spir·ing.**

jew·el (jü′əl), **1** a precious stone; gem. Jewels are used in the moving parts of some watches, as well as worn in pins and other ornaments. **2** a valuable ornament to be worn, often made of gold or silver and set with gems. **3** to set or decorate with jewels or with things like jewels. **1,2** *noun,* **3** *verb.*

loot (lüt), **1** to rob; plunder. **2** things taken by force; booty; spoils. **1** *verb,* **2** *noun.*

mar·ble (mär′bəl), **1** a hard limestone, white or colored, that can take a beautiful polish. Marble is much used for statues and in buildings. **2** made of marble: *a marble floor*. **3** a small, usually colored glass ball, used in children's games. 1,3 *noun*, 2 *adjective*.

may·or (mā′ər), a person at the head of a city or town government. *noun*.

mer·chant (mėr′chənt), **1** a person who buys and sells goods for a living. **2** a storekeeper. **3** trading, having something to do with trade: *merchant ships*. 1,2 *noun*, 3 *adjective*.

mosque (mosk), a Moslem place of worship. *noun*.

mosque

nee·dle·work (nē′dl wėrk′), work done with a needle; sewing; embroidery.

par·boil (pär′boil′), to boil till partly cooked. *verb*.

pier (pir), **1** a structure built out over the water, and used as a walk or a landing place. **2** one of the solid supports on which the arches of a bridge rest; pillar. *noun*.

pi·ña·ta (pē nyä′tə), a pot filled with candy, fruit, and small toys, hung at Christmas time in Mexico and other Latin American countries. Blindfolded children swing sticks in order to break the pot to get what is inside. *noun*, *plural* **pi·ña·tas**.

pot·ter·y (pot′ər ē), pots, dishes, or vases made from clay and hardened by heat. *noun*.

pre·dic·a·ment (pri dik′ə mənt), an unpleasant, difficult, or bad situation: *She was in a predicament when she missed the last train home. noun*.

pros·pec·tor (pros′pek tər), a person who explores or examines a region, searching for gold, silver, oil, uranium, or other valuable resources. *noun*.

ru·in (rü′ən), **1** Often, **ruins**, *plural*, that which is left after a building or wall has fallen to pieces: *the ruins of an ancient city*. **2** very great damage; destruction; overthrow. **3** a fallen or decayed condition: *The house had gone to ruin from neglect*. **4** the cause of destruction, decay, or downfall: *Reckless spending will be your ruin*. **5** to destroy; spoil. 1-4 *noun*, 5 *verb*.

sab·o·tage (sab′ə täzh), **1** damage done to property, machinery, bridges, railroads, or the like, especially by enemy agents. *noun*.

shel·ter (shel′tər), **1** something that covers or protects from weather, danger, or attack. **2** to protect; shield; hide: *to shelter runaway slaves*. **3** protection; refuge. **4** a temporary place of shelter for poor or homeless people, or for animals without owners. 1,3,4 *noun*, 2 *verb*.

slack (slak), **1** not tight or firm; loose: *a slack rope.* **2** the part that hangs loose: *Pull in the slack of the rope.* **3** slow. 1,3 *adjective*, 2 *noun.*

square knot, a knot firmly joining two loose ends of rope or cord. Each end is formed into a loop which both encloses and passes through the other.

square knot

a	hat	i	it	oi	oil	ch	child	ə stands for:
ā	age	ī	ice	ou	out	ng	long	a in about
ä	far	o	hot	u	cup	sh	she	e in taken
e	let	ō	open	ù	put	th	thin	i in pencil
ē	equal	ô	order	ü	rule	ᴛʜ	then	o in lemon
ėr	term					zh	measure	u in circus

tie-dye (tī/dī/), dye (cloth) by tying some of the material in knots to prevent the cloth inside from absorbing the dye. *verb,* **tie-dyed, tie·dy·ing.**

tram·ple (tram/pəl), **1** to walk or step heavily on; crush. **2** to walk or step heavily; tramp. *verb,* **tram·ples, tram·pled, tram·pling.**

stock (stok), **1** things for use or for sale; supply used as it is needed: *The store keeps a large stock of toys.* **2** cattle or other farm animals; livestock: *The farm was sold with all its stock.* **3** to lay in a supply of; supply: *Our camp is well stocked with food.* **4** to get or keep regularly for use or for sale. **5** kept on hand regularly for use or for sale. **6** a part used as a support or handle: *the stock of a rifle.* 1,2,6 *noun*, 3,4 *verb*, 5 *adjective.*

sus·pi·cious (sə spish/əs), **1** causing one to suspect: *Someone suspicious was hanging around the house.* **2** feeling suspicion; suspecting. *adjective.*

tem·ple (tem/pəl), **1** a building used for the service or worship of a god or gods. **2** any building set apart for worship, especially a Jewish synagogue. *noun.*

weigh (wā), **1** to find out how heavy a thing is. **2** to have as a measure by weight: *I weigh 110 pounds.* **3** to bend by weight; burden: *boughs weighed down with fruit.* **4** to bear down; be a burden. **5** to balance in the mind; consider carefully: *He weighs his words before speaking.* **6** to lift up an anchor. *verb.*

wor·ship (wėr/ship), **1** great honor and respect: *the worship of God.* **2** to pay great honor and respect to. **3** ceremonies or services in honor of God. Prayers and hymns are part of worship. **4** to take part in a religious service. **5** to consider extremely precious; hold very dear; adore: *A miser worships money.* 1,3 *noun*, 2,4,5 *verb.*

Acknowledgments

Text

Page 6: *Something Queer in Rock 'n' Roll* by Elizabeth Levy. Text copyright © 1987 by Elizabeth Levy. Illustrations copyright © 1987 by Mordicai Gerstein. Used by permission of Dell Books, a division of Bantam Doubleday Dell Publishing Group, Inc.

Page 26: "The Crow and the Pitcher" from *Belling the Cat and Other Aesop's Fables* retold in verse by Tom Paxton, illustrated by Robert Rayevsky. Copyright © 1990 by Tom Paxton. Illustrations copyright © 1990 by Robert Rayevsky. Reprinted by permission of William Morrow & Company, Inc.

Page 28: "How to Weigh an Elephant" from *Pebbles From a Broken Jar* by Frances Alexander. Copyright © 1963, 1967 by Frances Alexander. Reprinted with permission of Macmillan Publishing Company, a Division of Macmillan, Inc.

Page 30: "Bo Rabbit Smart for True" from *Bo Rabbit Smart for True* retold by Priscilla Jaquith, illustrated by Ed Young. Text copyright © 1981 by Priscilla Jaquith, illustrations copyright © 1981 by Ed Young. Reprinted by permission of Philomel Books.

Page 38: "Mother Goose Gumshoe" by Christina Hamlett, *Plays*, October 1987, pp. 35–38. Copyright © 1987 by Plays, Inc. Reprinted by permission.

Page 48: From the book *Family Pictures:* paintings and stories by Carmen Lomas Garza, as told to Harriet Rohmer. Copyright © 1990 by Carmen Lomas Garza. Reprinted by permission of GRM Associates, Agents for Children's Book Press.

Page 60: "Faith Ringgold's Stories in Art," by Leslie Sills. Copyright © by Leslie Sills, 1991.

Page 68: "Pad and Pencil" from *One at a Time* by David McCord. Copyright © 1965, 1966 by David McCord. Reprinted by permission of Little, Brown and Company.

Page 70: *The Boll Weevil* verses selected and illustrated by Glen Rounds. Copyright © 1967 by Glen Rounds. Reprinted by permission of Childrens Press, Chicago, Illinois.

Page 80: "The Traveling Sign Painters," by Glen Rounds. Copyright © by Glen Rounds, 1991.

Page 84: *Mr. Yowder and the Train Robbers*, text and illustrations by Glen Rounds. Copyright © 1981 by Glen Rounds. Reprinted by permission of Holiday House. All rights reserved.

Page 108: *Roxaboxen* by Alice McLerran, illustrated by Barbara Cooney. Text copyright © 1991 by Alice McLerran. Illustrations copyright © 1991 by Barbara Cooney. Reprinted by permission of Lothrop, Lee & Shepard Books, a division of William Morrow & Company, Inc.

Page 124: "My Dress Is Old" from *Dancing Teepees: Poems of American Indian Youth.* Text reprinted by permission of Friendship Press. Illustration reprinted by permission of Holiday House. Illustration copyright © 1989 by Stephen Gammell. All rights reserved.

Page 125: "I Watched an Eagle Soar" by Virginia Driving Hawk Sneve from *Dancing Teepees: Poems of American Indian Youth* selected by Virginia Driving Hawk Sneve. Copyright © 1989 by Virginia Driving Hawk Sneve. Illustration copyright © 1989 by Stephen Gammell. All rights reserved.

Reprinted by permission of Holiday House.

Page 126: From *Round Buildings, Square Buildings, & Buildings That Wiggle Like a Fish* by Philip M. Isaacson. Copyright © 1988 by Philip M. Isaacson. Reprinted by permission of Alfred A. Knopf, Inc.

Page 132: "Buildings Are Restless," by Philip M. Isaacson. Copyright © by Philip M. Isaacson, 1991.

Artists

Illustrations owned and copyrighted by the illustrator.
Steven Guarnaccia cover, 1–5, 135–139
Mordicai Gerstein 6–25
Robert Rayevsky 26–27
Charles Liu 28–29
Ed Young 30–37
Robert Dale 38–47
Carmen Lomas Garza 48–59
Lilla Rogers 68–69
Glen Rounds 70–79, 84–106
Jim Lange 107
Barbara Cooney 108–123
Stephen Gammell 124–125

Photographs

Unless otherwise acknowledged, all photographs are the property of Scott Foresman.
Page 60: Faith Ringgold, *Sonny's Quilt,* 1986. Acrylic on canvas, tie-dyed, printed and pieced fabrics—84½″ × 60″. Collection Bernice Steinbaum Gallery, NYC.
Page 63: (left) Faith Ringgold, *Aunt Edith,* 1974. Acrylic on canvas, fabric yarn, beads, raffia, foam—64″ × 19″ × 13″. Family of Woman Mask Series. Courtesy Bernice Steinbaum Gallery, NYC. Photo by Karen Bell. (center) Faith Ringgold, *Aunt Bessie,* 1974. Acrylic on canvas, fabric, yarn, beads, raffia, foam—65½″ × 19″ × 12″. Family of Woman Mask Series. Courtesy Bernice Steinbaum Gallery, NYC. Photo by Karen Bell. (right) Faith Ringgold, *Martin Luther King, Jr.,* 1975. Acrylic on canvas, fabric, wig hair, beads, embroidery, foam—62½″ × 8″ × 19″; life size portrait mask. Courtesy Bernice Steinbaum Gallery, NYC.
Page 65: Faith Ringgold, *Tar Beach,* 1988. Acrylic on canvas, painted, pieced, printed fabrics—74″ × 69″. Collection: Solomon R. Guggenheim Museum, NYC. Courtesy Bernice Steinbaum Gallery, NYC.
Page 67: Faith Ringgold with detail of "The Purple Quilt." Courtesy Bernice Steinbaum Gallery, NYC. Photo by C. Love, 1986.
Page 81: Courtesy Glen Rounds
Page 82: Division of Manuscripts/University of Oklahoma Library
Page 83: The Bancroft Library, University of California, Berkeley
Pages 127–131: Philip M. Isaacson
Page 132: Karen Vander
Pages 133–134: Courtesy Philip M. Isaacson
Page 140: (left) USDA
Page 142: Walter S. Clarke, Jr.

Glossary

The contents of the glossary have been adapted from *Beginning Dictionary,* Copyright © 1988 Scott, Foresman and Company.